# WALKS ON SCOTTISH LOWLAND HILLS

## 22 UNUSUAL ROUTES ILLUSTRATED

## MIKE NEWBURY

ISBN  978-0-9545227-1-1

*By the same author*
## *Walks and Scrambles in the Julian Alps*
## *based on Kranjska Gora*
*Zlatorog Publications*

## Acknowledgements

The author thanks his faithful companions on the hill,
Gordon Gove and Dougal Roy,
also Sarah and Laura Newbury, Robert and Thomas Hancock
for their participation, and Pat Newbury for her longtime support.
The author thanks Dougal Roy for checking text and design - any remaining
errors lie with the author.

ISBN 978-0-9545227-1-1

Cartography and technical assistance by Helen Stirling Maps, Inverness
(www.helenstirlingmaps.com).
All route maps: Reproduced by permission of Ordnance Survey on behalf of HMSO,
© Crown copyright 2012. All rights reserved. Ordnance Survey Licence no.100052343.

Printed by
G. H. Smith & Son www.ghsmith.com

All photos by the author unless otherwise attributed.

# Contents

# Key to the route maps

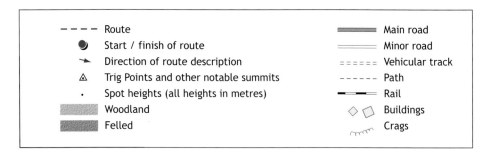

Cover photos:
Front: Looking over Snout Hill from Mathieside Cairn, on the return from Broad Law.
Back: Talla Cleuch Head from Games Hope.

# Introduction

These routes are scattered between the Sidlaws in the north-east and the Moffat hills in the south. None are beyond the Highland Line, or where would they end? I apologise to Edinburgh and Glasgow readers for omitting hills to the east and west - being confined by the size of this book to a selection of 22 routes, I have restricted myself to the best of those familiar to me. I am sorry, also, that there is nothing in wild Galloway.

I have avoided popular routes up popular hills - they are over-described and over-trodden already. Rather, I have described lesser-used routes, or routes of my own devising, which are mostly easy underfoot, using grass tracks and paths where available - usually the double wheel marks of ATVs (All Terrain Vehicles) used by shepherds (and their dogs!) The pastures are normally sufficiently robust for these tracks not to be obtrusive, but be warned that if underused they may fade and become hard to find. I have generally avoided heathery moors, with their peat hags and tracks ripped through the peat for grouse shooting. On Pykestone Hill and Broad Law, however, I have included fairly well landscaped vehicular hill tracks to gain height and position for a more challenging return route.

The routes are nearly all moderate. Some have potential dangers (minor by mountaineering standards) to which I hope I have drawn sufficient attention. One is distinctly different - the Elie Chain Walk - and is included for its intrinsic interest and to correct misleading comparisons with an alpine *via ferrata*.

The routes are nearly all circular from access points because, of course, the use of a car is assumed! This is distinctly not 'green', but the infrequency of convenient public transport and the misery of walking along roads suffering the noise and danger of passing traffic, make this practically unavoidable.

The greatest of guidebook writers, Alfred Wainwright, says in *Fellwanderer* (Westmorland Gazette Ltd. Kendal 1966) 'When you step off the tarmacadam on to the rough ground, danger is past, not just beginning.' He gives detailed advice on careful foot placement, and says in conclusion, 'Don't forget to watch where you are putting your feet, and you'll be all right'. But accidents do happen, usually on the descent, when concentration flags - and if you sprain an ankle when on most of the walks in this book, there's less likelihood of anyone coming to help than on a popular Munro - you may well see no-one all day. Such solitude is ideal for the solo walker to exercise self-reliance in relatively tame circumstances, and enjoy intense empathy with surrounding nature.

As one who travels light, I hesitate to advise on what to carry. With experience, some choice of gear becomes automatic - walking boots, fleece top, wind/waterproofs, plus hat and gloves in winter, with some spares. In T-shirt and shorts weather, carry at least a lightweight windproof. Have a change of clothing in the car. Take food and drink. Map and compass should also be automatic, and head-torch in winter. Walking poles (I use Pacerpoles) enhance stability and save knees from wear. Crampons are for hard snow (practise first, so they don't trip you up) and ice axe for snow on steep ground. Beware hard snow patches, and  exhausting snow-drifts.  Remember that a retreat or an escape route may be needed.

The times stated for each route are generous - a few years ago, I would have laughed at them, and hard walkers are welcome to do so now! I hope they are consistent, so that personal times may be forecast after sampling.

Many walkers, particularly those coming from an English background, may be unaware of their rights of access. The Scottish law is the converse of the English - instead of being allowed **only** on specific routes and areas, the walker is allowed **anywhere except** on specific areas such as railways and private gardens, provided that he or she acts responsibly. The land owner or manager also has responsibilities, e.g. not to allow land operations to unduly obstruct walkers. All these rights and responsibilities are spelt out in the Scottish Outdoor Access Code. (ISBN 1-853197-422-6) available from Scottish Natural Heritage www.snh.org.uk

Remember that cattle are a law to themselves. Cows with calves may see you and especially your dog, if you have one, as a threat, and attack you. Dogs should normally be kept 'under close control' but if cattle approach, you must let your dog go free. More usually, cattle are placid, and they are a consideration at the beginning and end of only a few of these routes.

I have taken care in my descriptions, but errors remain possible, and features such as paths and fences are liable to change. I hope readers will understand that I must make the usual disclaimer, namely that I take no responsibility for accidents or mishaps to users of this book, however caused.

This book is intended to provide for moderate walkers, including those like me of diminished powers, and to encourage those, especially beginners, who are nervous of leaving well-trodden ways. I hope that all the routes in this book will be found interesting, but that I am not exposing hidden gems to over-intrusion (or worse, erosion) - they should remain the preserve of the discriminating!

# 1.          Benarty, Fife

## Character
This is a splendid short outing on a steep little hill, which rises precipitously to the south of Loch Leven and to the east of the M90. The walk is mainly through woodland, but the summit is on a rough open plateau above crags.

## Summary

| | | | |
|---|---|---|---|
| **Distance:** | 4 miles | **Height gained:** | 230m |
| **Time:** | 2.5 hours | **Map:** | O.S. Landranger 58 |

**Start and finish:** Car park at the north-west corner of Lochore. GR 158 959. Leave the M90 at Junction 4, drive straight through Kelty to the end, and take the B996 north; turn right after 1 mile along the second minor road for Lochore Meadows Country park and stop after 1 mile at the landscaped car park before a barrier across the road.

*The gate*

## Route
Walk back along the road for a few metres, and turn right, through a gate on to a broad track which slants to the right up Harran Hill within the edge of mature deciduous woodland.

*Loch Ore from the start of the track*

The track steepens and swings left past rocks, then levels and swings right; and then through another gate.

Here you turn left past an information signboard. Then walk on, past a barrier, and cross a tarred public road.

*Turn left here*

*On the steps*

Take the steep path into deep forest up flights of 190 steps with timber risers, trending right then left and right again.

Join a grassy track, benched into the hillside through more open woodland and rising gently to the left.

The track ends in an unmade footpath traversing through mature conifers.

*The traversing path*

*The grassy track*

Then the path swings up right on slabby bedrock, then out of the forest over a low wire fence and remains of a dike on to moorland.

8

Continue close to the forest through turf, heather and blaeberry, swing up sharply to the left and follow the narrow worn path through heather to a little knoll rising from the plateau.

*Turn right up slabby bedrock*

*Continue close to the forest*

The path continues north-west on a swinging undulating line for another 400m or so, to reach the summit Trig. pillar at 356m. It is best to stop a few metres further on, near the edge of the crags, to enjoy the dramatic views over Loch Leven.

*The crags looking westwards*

*The summit*

Continue on a rough grass track winding down through knolls of heather and blae-berry to a saddle, with the steep drop beyond a semi-derelict dike and fence to the right, and more gentle slopes to the left.

*The path down to the saddle*

It is possible to continue up the steep rise on the other side, then along a ridge of rocky knolls, but this involves crossing an awkward fence and then a steep rough descent followed by fields.

It is easier to turn left in the saddle, and down a sketchy grass path to a gate in a deer fence.

Go through the gate and down a vehicular track through native woodland planting. At a 'T' junction turn right.

*Start of the vehicular track*

*The vehicular track*

At the lower end of the plantation, there is a locked gate with an unlocked pedestrian gate to the right.

The track continues downhill into a large open field, then fades, and resumes in the far left hand corner to finish at a gate on to the tarred road which was crossed on the way up.

*Into the field*

*Out of the field*

Turn right along the road for a few metres, then left through an imposing gateway, and almost immediately right, off the main tarred drive, and gently down a vehicular track with policy woodland on the left, and fields on the right.

Pass a substantial farmhouse and farm buildings on the left, and along an almost level road in an avenue of trees to reach the public road at a 'T' junction, where you turn left, to reach the car park after about 800m.

The gateway

The finish

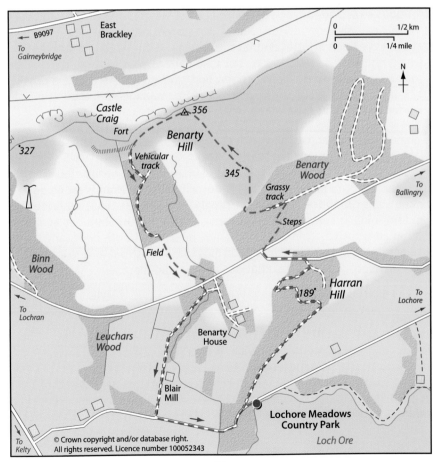

# 2.      The Elie Chain Walk

## Character

This is a famous walk requiring cautionary notes! It is not properly a hillwalk: its essence is a scramble round sea cliffs, with fixed chains at points of difficulty. It is tide-dependent - avoid High Water by at least 2 hours and note that there is no safe escape up the cliffs which are steep, and in their upper sections loose and dangerous. Check website 'NTSLF - Tidal predictions for Leith' noting that the times given are for Greenwich Mean Time.

The route is often compared to an Alpine *via ferrata*, but the chains are less amenable to *via ferrata* style protection with karabiners than the taut steel cables and fixed pegs well known to me in the Julian Alps (see penultimate photo); and as they hang loose and sagging, using them on the steeper rock is a **strenuous exercise**. Anyone of limited power-against-weight should **beware**. The rocks are not generally far below, but potentially damaging nonetheless, and there have been injuries and fatalities here. A 'fun-walk' for energetic (but not small) children, and fit adults, but take care of your footing, particularly if the rock is wet, and when on the chain, **don't let go!** There is also a possibility of rock-fall. Alpine *via ferrata* are far more manageable than the chains, though far longer, and much more liable to objective dangers.

The chains vary in length from 10 feet to 50 feet. They were first installed in the late 1920s and replaced recently in stainless steel. There are 5 short chains more or less vertical, and 3 long chains more or less horizontal. The chain section can be done either way, but is **described here from west to east, and the chains are numbered here accordingly**. The whole walk is described starting and finishing at Earlsferry (to the east), with a note of Shell Bay at the other end as an alternative. There are fine sandy beaches at both ends, and the walk over Kincraig Point to make the circuit has fine views, but is decorated by the ruins of concrete wartime installations and a radio mast.

## Summary

**Distance:**      3 miles (Chain Walk: 1/3 mile)
**Time:**      3 hours (Chain Walk: 1 hour)
**Map:**      O.S. Landranger 59
**Start and finish:** Limited marked on-street parking at the west end of Earlsferry High St, or nearby unmarked on-street (avoiding nuisance or illegality). GR 481997. Alternative: Council Car park at entrance to Shell Bay caravan site. GR 469005.

# Route

From the west end of Earlsferry High Street, cross Links Road and walk a few metres along Chapel Green Road, then fork right along a broad path crossing a corner of the golf course, noting the danger of golf balls from both directions. On reaching the shore, join the official Fife Coastal Path (after it has diverted round a headland) and turn west on the official path following the strip of sand dune between the golf course and the foreshore.

*Start of the path*

*Looking back up the path from the shore*

View of the end (or start) of the chain walk from the junction with the Fife Coastal Path

*The coastal path rises from the shore*

*The coastal path above Kincraig Point*

At a signpost, take the clear Fife Coastal Path rising up a steep grass slope first to the right, then to the left, to the crest leading to the Trig. pillar (63m) and radio mast above Kincraig Point.

Descend gently to the west, then down the first of two flights of steps and look for a signboard on a clump of rocks away down towards the sea.

Turn off the clear way, down a steep sketchy path through turf (which may be slippery in wet or icy weather) to reach the signboard confirming the start of the Chain Walk proper.

*The sketchy path*

*The signboard*

# Elie Chainwalk
## WARNING

This unique scramble will take you across hazardous coastal terrain for 0.5 Km.
There are 8 chains, some vertical, with up to 10 metres height gain/loss. Allow 1-3 Hours.

Beware of the following risks to yourself and others with you:

**BECOMING TRAPPED BY THE INCOMING TIDE -**
**the slopes above are very steep, loose and dangerous to climb.**

**BEING STRUCK BY FALLING STONES AND ROCK.**

**FALLING FROM STEEP ROCK -**
Secure hand and foot grip is essential, particularly when wet.

If you are wearing suitable clothing and footwear and decide to proceed,
please do so with great care.

**Fife**
COUNCIL

**Email feedback:** chain.walk@fife.gov.uk   www.fifedirect.org.uk/chainwalk

Follow the slight path over rocky ground eastwards to a steel post on a crest of rock. Grasp the post, turn round, and facing inwards, put toes in the pockets cut into the rock, transfer hands to the chain, and down you go! The rock is not steep, but to face outwards is to risk a tumble. (This is Chain No. 1 from the west)

*Robert Hancock on Chain No. 2*

14

Chain No. 3

Descend slabby rock and cross the mouth of a cave to gain a horizontal chain (No 2 from the west) above a ledge or footholds - in balance, so that it can be followed comfortably.

Immediately after, ascend a longer vertical chain - indeed it is undercut at the base, but the pockets are good - pull over the crest using the steel post. (Chain No 3)

Then down a short chain (No. 4 from the west) on slabby then undercut rock - it may be difficult to find the pockets here, leaning out on a swinging chain, as against the fixed pegs of an Alpine 'equipped' route.

Chain No. 4

Chain No. 5

The bouldery beach

Next, walk along a bouldery beach past a nose of rock, then on sand and shingle and over large boulders past 'organ-pipes' of rock to a huge rock of pudding-stone leaning against the crag which is here a steep slab, undercut at the base. There is a line of pockets, with a hanging chain. Climb this, strenuously at first, and step to the right to a steel post planted in the gap.

15

Descend a short hanging chain (No 6) over large pockets to a black pebble beach.

At the end of the beach, scramble round the slabby base of the cliff, undercut at first, and on grassy ledges pass above a natural arch.

Arrive at a rock saddle, from which a chain (No. 7 from the west) leads diagonally down above a wide but broken ledge, ending abruptly above a

*Chain No. 7*

Chain No. 6

*The scrambling traverse*

rock fissure, which you must step over, supported by the hanging end of the chain. Step down, and cross the boulders at the end of the sea inlet to Chain No 8.

Chain No. 8

*For comparison:- security on tight cable with 2 karabiners attached to belt. Laura Newbury on Mala Mojstrovka, Slovenia*

Pull up on this last chain, to traverse on pockets below an overhang - the downward and outward pull on the slack chain and the incut pockets below force weight onto arms and shoulders - keep moving! Then pull round a corner to the end of the chain above huge steps.

**Note**: Except near full tide, it is possible to avoid this chain by walking along the top of the beach.

Continue on rocky then grassy terraces, pass the warning sign (identical with the sign at the west end) and continue on or above the fine sandy beach, to re-join the outward walk on the strip of dune between the golf course and the foreshore.

*End of Chain No. 8*

## Alternative start from Shell Bay

Turn south off the A917 at GR 469 005, and after about 1 mile, after passing through woodland, turn right into an enclosed Council Car Park. Then either -

(a) walk 1/3 mile along the tarred road which follows the perimeter of the caravan site, turn left over a footbridge close to the sea, and take the Fife Coastal Path eastwards, turning down the steep path to the warning sign immediately after the first flight of steps, or

(b) take the uphill track towards the radio mast and turn left almost at the end, up a grass path and through a gate to the signed Fife Coastal Path close to the mast. Descend to find the warning sign as described for the Earlsferry start.

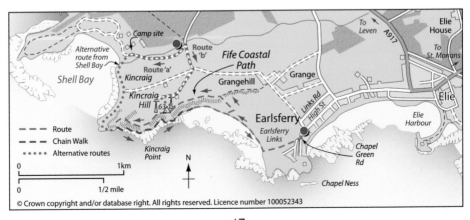

# 3.  Sidlaws - Auchterhouse Hill and Craigowl

## Character
These hills form the central part of the Sidlaw range which separates the Firth of Tay from Strathmore, and rise immediately behind the northern outskirts of Dundee. They carry spoil from abandoned shallow quarries, and on Craigowl, large telephone and navigation installations. There is some picturesque woodland, and extensive recent plantings of native trees.

## Summary
**Distance:**    5 miles     **Height gained:**    420m
**Time:**    3 hours     **Map:**    O.S. Landranger 54
**Start and finish:** Balkello Community Woodland car park, 2 miles east along the Tealing road from Kirkton of Auchterhouse. Large car park, presently free, but note closing times. GR 365 384.

## Route
From the north-west corner of the car park follow the avenue rising to north-west through a plantation of native trees. Bear left at a fork, through a break in a dike, then take the middle of 3 ways continuing the same way to the top of an open rise below a power line, and note the track rising to right up the steep hillside ahead.

*Start of the route*

Cross the stone wall at the corner using a stone stile, and ascend the sloping track, which swings straight up the hill to a gate in a fence corner. Take the obvious track to left of the gate.

*Line of the sloping track*

*Grass track to the brow*   *The fork in the track and summit of Auchterhouse Hill*

Then continue up the track swinging gradually to the left, rising more gently over the brow to a sharp bend to the right with extensive views up the Firth of Tay. Follow the track to the right and sharp left again, then dipping a little towards open larch woodland rising steeply towards the summit of Auchterhouse Hill (426m). Take the left fork in the track and ascend northwards over the embankments of an extensive prehistoric fort to the summit

*The track rising over to Bulluderon Hill*

From the summit descend eastwards down a path through open woodland, and rejoin the track at the fork. Return down the track to where a narrow path appears on the left, before the sharp bend. Take this path, steeply down into a deep dip, step through a gate, and climb the steep eroded track rising over the brow of Balluderon Hill.

*The Scroggie Memorial Cairn*
*Photo: Peter Davidson*

The path gradually levels to the summit and the viewpoint indicator, a fine memorial inscribed to Sydney Scroggie, local worthy and 'man o' the hills'.

From the indicator, take the narrow path north, which joins the fence and runs level alongside, then dips sharply into a gap.

*The summit of Craigowl Hill*

*The direct approach*

Here, another fence with a gate forms a T junction. From the gate, the path rises, steeply at first, to Craigowl Hill (455m).

This hill is crowned by 2 massive sets of telecommunication and navigation installations each within high wire fences which are approached by a rough path rising through deep heather. The summit is marked by a Trig. pillar standing on a little grassy knoll between the 2 sets of installations.

The direct approach to the pillar is over a stile to the right of the first high enclosure. Pass this enclosure, then step over a low dilapidated fence to the pillar.

Begin the descent by returning to the stile, then bear left on a gently descending grass path.

A distant solitary house appears, straight ahead.

*Bear left for the descent*

*The Trig. pillar looking north*

As it descends, the path, which is faint in places, keeps fairly close to the main hillside with some low humps to the left.

20

Follow this line carefully. Finally, on level ground, approach a barbed wire fence and squeeze carefully between the fence and a patch of gorse for a few metres to a concealed gate in the fence.

*The line of descent*

*The squeeze*

*From the gate*

Go through the gate, and continue diagonally leftward through the trees until a broad track is reached. Cross this track, and following the same line (with the beacon of the solitary house appearing ahead from time to time) continue on a narrow steeply undulating stony track with steep rough ground and quarry faces above on the right until a well-used level track is joined.

*The stony track and the solitary house*

*The junction*

*The steep little path*

*The mown track*

Almost immediately, cut down to the left using a steep little path through dense bushes and trees.

Coming out of the bushes, continue on a wide mown track, then turn right through the plantation, and emerging on to the main track, turn left to the start.

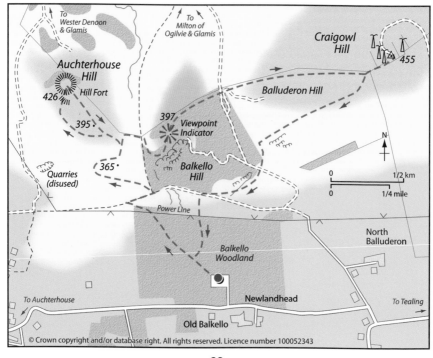

# 4.    Ochils - The Round of Glen Sherup

## Character
A fine and quiet walk, mostly on good grass tracks with gentle gradients, above pleasant countryside, and with views of the edge of the Highlands. Good for dogs, because it is all FCS or Woodland Trust except areas on Whitewisp and Tarmangie and the farm of Wester Glensherup. Interesting native woodland plantings, mainly birch, which are currently at small sapling stage, and grouped loosely with open spaces. Try to ignore the wind farms to east and north-west!

## Summary
| | | | |
|---|---|---|---|
| **Distance:** | 9 miles | **Height gained:** | 580m |
| **Time:** | 4.5 hours | **Map:** | O.S. Landranger 58 |
| | | | Harvey - Ochil Hills |

**Start and finish:** Forestry Commission car park & picnic area on the Muckhart - Gleneagles road. GR 973 052.

## Route
From the car park, ascend the forestry road. Passing above the Sherup dam, take the left fork and follow the road to the sign and cairn just beyond the present edge of the felling, where the road levels, and turn right at the sign, up an initially steep ride, and out through a gate.

*The ride under snow*                     *The edge of the forest looking east*

*The ascent of Innerdownie*                              *Summit*

Turn right (west) to follow the grass track up Inner-downie (611m).

23

Continue through a long dip, and up to a ladder stile. On the way up there was a nasty deep ditch to cross, but thankfully, the Woodland Trust have placed an unobtrusive footbridge over it.

From the ladder stile continue on the path to the summit cairn of Whitewisp (643m).

*Tarmangie from Innerdownie*

Turn sharp right towards Tarmangie (645m) and follow the trodden path into a dip, then a double grass track by a fence.

Cross through a gate to the Tarmangie summit path. A hollow on top usually provides shelter.

*The summit of Tarmangie*

*The gradual descent. Ben Shee to left*

*Stuc a'Chroin and Ben Vorlich from the descent ridge*

Follow the ridge path and turn down beside a wall and fence to a stile. Take the track to the right, indistinct at first. (The track to the left provides a good 'high-level' route to Ben Cleuch and back, passing over the north shoulder of Andrew Gannel.)

Ascend slightly, then make a gradual descent of the broad ridge on a grass track (boggy patches if wet). On a clear day there are good views of the Highland edge.

Follow the track past the lowest point of the depression before the hump of Ben Shee. Continue by a vehicular track over the shoulder of Ben Shee, then down to a tarred road, and continue the descent to the main road. Turn right and find the car park in about 400m.

*Glensherup Reservoir from the zigzags*

Alternatively, take the grassy zigzags down from the start of the depression and follow a near-level track (part of it sloping sideways) past the fishermen's car park to the dam, then cross the dam, climb a bank to the forestry road, and descend to the car park.

This walk is suitable for mist, rain, and snow, but note that the rise to Innerdownie can take a heavy accumulation of snow.

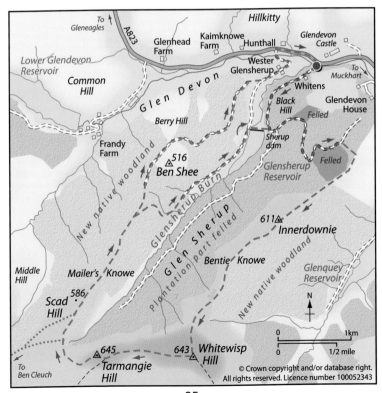

25

# 5.  Ochils - Wood Hill

## Character

This walk is convenient for a short expedition from Tillicoultry, or, using either the ascent or descent, as a way to or from Ben Cleuch. The ascent is challengly steep in places. The route is little used, except near its start and finish.

## Summary

| | | | |
|---|---|---|---|
| **Distance:** | 5 miles | **Height gained:** | 455m |
| **Time:** | 3 hours | **Map:** | O.S. Landranger 58 |
| | | | Harvey: Ochil Hills |

**Start and finish:** Mill Glen, Tillicoultry.  GR 914 976.

## Route

Drive up the Mill Glen road in Tillicoultry, past the Woolpack Inn, to the small parking area, or (better, I think) drive over the bridge and park by the grass opposite the houses. Walk along the street to the west, down a little, then turn right, up a broad path, and then down a little cut to the broad path signed for Alva, which heads west past the golf course. Shortly after entering a wood owned by the Woodland Trust, ascend a few metres to a parallel path, then, by a huge laurel, cut up a very steep lightly trodden path to reach an engineered east-west path which undulates high up across the steep wooded slope. Follow this path and traverse on a sketchy path from where the main path makes its final descent. Go over the disused fence and up and along through deep bracken to a sharp turning up a steep rise and the top of the wood.

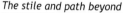

*The stile and path beyond*

*Looking back into the wood, with Alva below*

Cross a stile, then steeply up the grass slope, and traverse left, with two very short very steep sections of path rising from the traverses.

Then follow a rising traverse left, swing right at the remains of a dike, ignore a grass track to the left, and cross a tiny dip to face a steep summit slope. Zigzag up this slope, reaching the crest immediately to the right of the outcropping rocks, and turn left to the summit cairn (526m).

*View over to Stuc a'Chroin & Ben Vorlich*

Continue north along the grass path (not the double track) past a pool and across a depression to look down into a steep rocky gully. Here I usually rest on the rocks in a high sheltered corner.

(To continue to **Ben Cleuch**, take a descending traverse to near the head of the gully, then a slanting path up the opposite side, and up turf to the top of a

*Looking back up the gully*

broad ridge. Then follow the path along the ridge over Ben Ever, down the dip, over a stile and up the worn path beside a fence, and slant off right to the summit.)

To return, carefully descend the steep gully side (better use turf than the slippery unstable stones) to the bottom, follow down, and then traverse off left immediately after the big scree patch. Traverse the turf slope. Cross a fence. Then look for a thin grass path descending directly down.

*The thin grass descent path*

Turn down this path (or near it – it is very slippery if wet or icy) to reach a broad ugly track descending to the left (east), into the Mill Glen.

Follow this track as it swings right and turn down to the left by a big cairn, down a well worn grass path through bracken to the quarry edge (warning sign). Turn steeply downhill for a few metres, then traverse left along an engineered path benched into the steep hillside, and down a short zigzag to the top of steps on the main Mill Glen path, and so down to the car.

*The broad track*

*Into Mill Glen, with view of the main path over to Blackford*

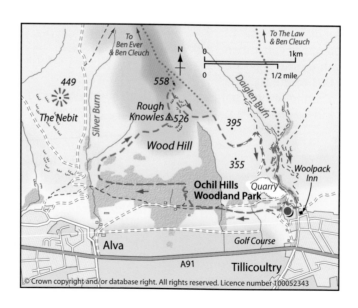

# 6.  Ochils - The Face of Dumyat

## Character
Dumyat ('Dum-aye-at') rises dramatically at the west end of the steep south-facing front line of the Ochils. It is only 418 metres high, but rocky. The main eroded route starts at a high point (183m) on the Sheriffmuir Road above Stirling University, and follows the crest of an escarpment. The selected route starts from a low level car park at Blairlogie, and ascends the steep face partly by way of a chasm; and on the return traverses the crags to the rough glen above Blairlogie. The traverse is **potentially dangerous**, especially when wet or icy, and the lower part of the ascent is strenuous. Either can be avoided by using a section of the main route (see below).

## Summary
| | | | |
|---|---|---|---|
| **Distance:** | 3 miles | **Height gained:** | 400m |
| **Time:** | 2.5 hours | **Map:** | O.S. Landranger 57 |
| | | | Harvey - Ochil Hills |

**Start and finish:** Car park at Blairlogie, on the Stirling - Menstrie road, GR 830 968.

## Route
From the back of the car park, cross the stile and turn right (eastwards). After a few metres, take a left fork (rising), and walk up a grassy bay in the gorse opposite a group of conifers. At the back of the bay, find a narrow worn path through the gorse trending up and right, then continue in the same direction on steep grass and bracken with outcropping mossy slabs and through gorse until the brink of a huge gully is reached.

*The grassy bay*

*Thomas Hancock on the steep grass and mossy slabs*

29

Follow the rising crest, then turn into the gully. The path is now narrow but clear.

The path crosses the gully and rises on the other side below crags.

The gully

The path runs below these crags

Upon coming out of the gully, take winding grass paths trending to the right, then steeply up to join the main path close to the rocky summit, which has been made unusually ugly but forms a fine viewpoint.

The summit

The start of the traverse

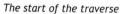

Return down to the gully head, and then carefully select, out of sketchy paths leading nowhere, the clear path rising to the right over a patch of slabby bedrock.

Continue horizontally, passing close below a steep rock.

Then more of the grass path follows interrupted by a patch of knobbly rock.

Now the path approaches the toe of the rock wall, and you must make a rising traverse over sloping but knobbly rock.

More traversing follows, on grass paths with small patches of easier rock to cross.

Then the route swings right, into a little gully, which is crossed at the head.

*The rising traverse over rock*

Now continue horizontally round a nose, and into a big gully, which is crossed on a steep earth path through gorse bushes.

*Into the little gully*

Then take a narrow traversing path leading over to the top of a broad slope descending into the wide valley above Blairlogie.

*The big gully*

Cross the valley to a rocky little stream-crossing and turn sharply downhill, over an open squelchy area, then through thick bushes and trees above the main stream in its gully.

*Turn sharply downhill*

31

Emerging on to open grass, head down left past a tank, cross the stream and traverse left on an overgrown path close to garden fences. Descend to a broad level track, and follow this to the left (east) to the stile behind the car park.

**To avoid the steep ascent**, reverse the descent to Blairlogie as far as the foot of the descent from the traverse of the crags (past the rocky little stream crossing) and then go straight up the shallow gully, to emerge suddenly on the skyline at the main path, which you follow to the summit. Then return by the route described.

*Start of descent to Blairlogie from main path*

**To avoid the traverse of the crags**, return from the summit on the main path as far as the shallow gully overlooking Blairlogie immediately before the fork in the main path and descend to Blairlogie. (see above)
I would not recommend going down the steep ascent route, as the outlook over warehouse roofs is painfully ugly - better facing the hillside!

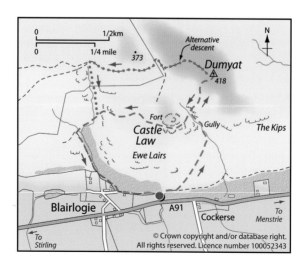

# 7.    Ochils – The Round of Glen Tye

## Character
A partly rough walk in bleak, wild country, with a high start, and a challenge finding the way! (Easiest when picked out by light snow. The penalty for minor errors is crossing tussocky ground, and for the worst error, finding yourself descending away down to Menstrie!) A (quiet) road walk of 2 miles is necessary to complete the circuit because tracks from intermediate points peter out.

## Summary
| | | | |
|---|---|---|---|
| **Distance:** | 11 miles | **Height gained:** | 450m |
| **Time:** | 4.5 hours | **Map:** | O.S. Landranger 57 & 58 |
| | | | Harvey – Ochil Hills |

**Start and finish:** Roadside, 800m south of Sheriffmuir Inn. GR 827 016.
Leave the car by the stream close to the signed 'weak bridge' where the road is widened on both sides. (Parking for a second car is feasible on a wide verge near the Greenloaning road junction.)

## Route
Walk up the road past Sheriffmuir Inn to the farm of Harperstone. Go through the gate on the right and almost immediately fork left – the required grass track is boggy and indistinct at first, but if you miss it, turn off the more obvi-

ous track (which goes the wrong way and stops) across patches of short grass to re-join the track before the gate close to the edge of the small conifer plantation. Go through the gate and follow the grass track straight up the rise to a small flat feeding area on the shoulder of Glentye Hill.

*The feeding area*

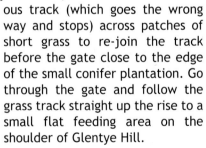

Ignore the continuation of the track to the summit and turn left along a traversing track bordered by rushes to a broad boggy saddle.

*The traversing track*

*To the fence on Mickle Corum*

Follow the track which turns across and towards Mickle Corum.

Then the track swings right, by-passing the summit, to a fence. The track now follows the fence along the broad ridge over Greenforet Hill

*Laura Newbury on Blairdenon.: View south*

to the summit of Blairdenon Hill, at 631m the second highest summit of the Ochils.

Descend south over rough ground – there are sketchy paths away from the fence.

*Descent to the Old Wharry Burn*

Cross the Old Wharry Burn close to the fence and climb the steep bank on the other side. Follow the fence over the rough and squelchy Menstrie Moss to reach a wall – which provides a dry seat!

*Crossing the Old Wharry Burn*

Follow the wall almost to a prominent bend. Here a grass track coming towards you from Colsnaur Hill, swings west in a quarter-circle, indistinct at first, but it should be clear by the time you are at right angles to the wall. Take this track.

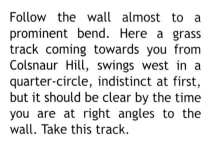

*Fork right!*

The track runs west, but winds about wildly. Ignore 2 forks to the left! There is a very minor fork right to ignore, but if in any doubt, check it out because it ends very soon in a feeding area on point 541. After a last wild swing left, the track swings right and downhill to a gate with huge posts.

The easiest way from here through the rough ground is to follow the electrified fence on its right side past the end of a shelter belt, then turn left through a gate and follow the far side of the trees through a pasture, then through another gate, down across the next field past the left hand end of a small plantation, through a gate, and round a barn and past a cottage to the road above the 'weak bridge'.

*The track swings downhill*

**Note – walk from Menstrie.**
This walk shares its middle east-west section with the round of Glen Tye, starting and finishing from Menstrie to the south.

Ascend the steep ugly zigzag track above the village and continue until it levels and crosses a stream, then turn off to the right up a grass track and follow it uphill, with some slight dips, until it swings north to pass before the summit slope of Colsnaur Hill, where you ascend the turf for a few metres to the cairn. (There is shelter in a nice quarry hole below the cairn.) Then north along the wall, and immediately after the bend, swing west along the track described above. Turn down left (track almost disappeared) at the top of the rise after crossing the big depression. Traverse west on rough ground and cross a sharp depression (wet) and up the other side to a good north-south track, which you follow south down to fields and the ruin of Jerah. Then a descending traverse across 2 fields to the Menstrie Glen, and a good scenic path, which rises to avoid a ravine, to traverse above the Glen and join the road at the top of the zigzags, where the outlook is over houses and industry. The rough crossing has the merit of a broad target in the north-south track.

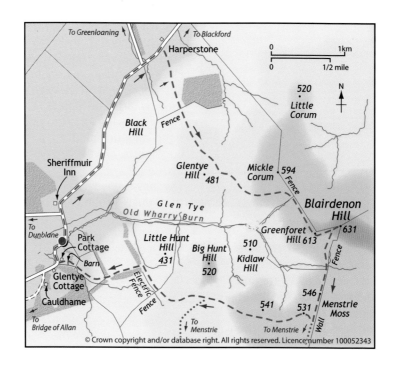

To Greenloaning

To Blackford

Harperstone

0        1km
0        1/2 mile

520
Little
Corum

N

Black
Hill

Fence

Sheriffmuir
Inn

Glentye
Hill · 481

Mickle
Corum

594

Fence

Blairdenon
Hill

Glen Tye
Old Wharry Burn

To
Dunblane

Park
Cottage

Barn

Little Hunt
Hill
· 431

Big Hunt
Hill
· 520

510
·

Kidlaw
Hill

Greenforet
Hill 613

631

Fence

Glentye
Cottage

Cauldhame

Electric Fence

Fence

546 ·

541 · 531 ·

Menstrie
Moss

Wall

Fence

To
Bridge of Allan

To
Menstrie

To Menstrie

# 8. Pentlands - Carlops by Monks Rig

## Character
Pleasant grassy ridges, with wide views over pastoral country.

## Summary

| | | | |
|---|---|---|---|
| Distance: | 7 miles | Height gained: | 300m |
| Time: | 3.5 hours | Map: | O.S. Landranger 65 |
| | | | Harvey - Pentland Hills |

**Start and finish:** Nine Mile Burn - turn off the A702 Edinburgh - Biggar road and park in a wide space opposite a row of cottages. GR 177 576.

## Route
Walk through the gate at the north end of the parking area, on the signed route for Balerno, and follow it up a steeply undulating grassy path. Continue uphill at a signed junction, and enter rough pasture by 2 stiles near a fence corner.

The way continues by a generally firm and dry grass path making a slight furrow (presumably formed by ancient usage) on a broad and gently undulating ridge, passing the Font Stone, a hollowed block once the base for a cross.

*On Monks Rig*

The sharp cone of West Kip (551m) comes into sight, and is prominent when Cap Law is reached (497m - the start of the walk being at 290m).

The route swings left in an arc round the head of Monks Burn, but by diverting straight ahead and dropping a little to the main Pentland watershed, West Kip may be climbed as an optional extra (because, like Everest, it is there)!

The route continues west, south-west and south as a double grass track, now less used and occasionally soggy, up to the rounded summit of Green Law (527m). It drops some 30m to a gate, then makes a gentle rise to the long top of Spittal Hill (526m).

*West Kip, East Kip & Scald Law from Cap Law*

Continue south beside a fence on a steepening grassy descent to suddenly reach a vehicular track crossing east-west. This provides a quick return past Spittal Farm to the minor road and car parking, but much better continue for the interesting finale of Patie's Hill (478m), a rise of some 30m up a grass track.

*Looking back on Green Law & Cap Law, with the Kips beyond, from Spittal Hill*

*The quick return track*

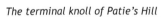

*The terminal knoll of Patie's Hill*

*The south ridge of Patie's Hill*

The broad ridge descending southwards from Patie's Hill undulates, then drops to a distinct saddle and rises to a steep terminal knoll. If you continue over this knoll you will have to descend steep bracken slopes to dubious paths above the North Esk stream. If you drop to the right from the saddle you will need to cross minor bogs and rock outcrops.

For a 'sensible' way down, take a rising traverse left, then horizontally over rough turf, and gently down past the end of a recently planted shelter belt to a gate into a field, signed as a public route.

*Descending to the field*  *Into the field*

Enter the field and follow down beside the fence to a gate, or if there is a problem with livestock in the field stay outside on rough rutted paths.

*Down the field*  *The rocky knoll*

Then take a path steeply down over rough ground to a gate by a rocky knoll into a narrow path outside a garden hedge. Enter a lane and cross a bridge past a 'scenic' house and mill stream, and out on to the main A702 at Carlops Bridge.

*View from the lane*

Turn left along a pavement over a bridge and after some 100m escape from the road, up steps to a footpath above the road and parallel to it, to join a minor road in about 400m. Then follow the minor road for about a mile to the car parking.

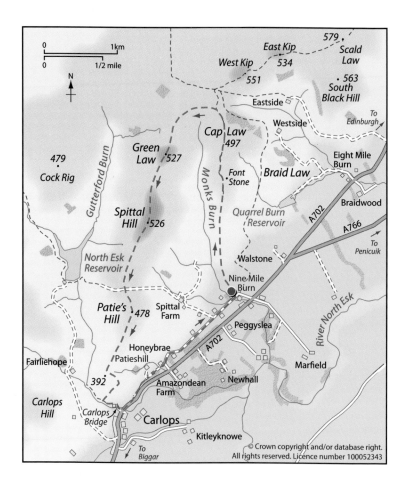

# 9. Pentlands - Mount Maw

## Character
A broad ridge of rough grassland with easy slopes, returning by farm tracks. Wide views over pastoral and moorland country.

## Summary

| | | | |
|---|---|---|---|
| **Distance:** | 9 miles | **Height gained:** | 300m |
| **Time:** | 4.5 hours | **Map:** | O.S. Landranger 72 |
| | | | Harvey - Pentland Hills |

**Start and finish:** Car Park at Carlops. GR 161 558. On the east side of the A702 road at the south end of the village, below a pinnacle of rock.

## Route

*Start and finish*

Walk a few metres south along the main road and turn right up a steep hill, then where the road turns left, continue straight ahead on an unsurfaced farm road which levels, then dips and makes a sharp turn right and steeply uphill to pass the farm buildings of Fairliehope on the right and a small plantation on the left. Once the brow of the hill is reached, turn off left on unfenced pasture and walk up to the top of the plantation, then continue up the broad ridge of Fairliehope Hill..

On the brow of the hill, the grass becomes tussocky: look out for a grass track (two wheelmarks) on the left, which carries you past the top of Fairliehope Hill (472m), over the left-hand side of the slight dip beyond, and up the final slope of The Mount (538m). This affords fine views of the Firth of Forth and the northern Pentlands.

*Fairliehope Hill, The Mount, and Grain Heads from Paties Hill. The route follows the green ridge, then the skyline.*

From the summit, two wheelmarks provide an intermittently squelchy route southwards along the broad crown of the ridge. There is a very slight dip and rise to Grain Heads (532m).

*Looking past Grain Heads to Mount Maw*

Then the ridge dips through boggy areas, and rises to Mount Maw (535m) on drier ground, with a clear track running along a fence. From the summit Trig. pillar follow the track south by a wall and fence, down a long broad ridge, to a sharp dip before the terminal knoll of Faw Mount.

*Mount Maw*

*Descending Mount Maw in winter*

Then, either continue on a grass track over Faw Mount, and cross a deep cleft with rock outcrops, or swing right to contour round Faw Mount on rough and in places wet ground.

*Cross the cleft, and turn left by the wall*

*Faw Mount*

Follow the left turn of the wall and down through pastures to reach an initially green farm track and public right-of-way.

If you have a car or cycle waiting on the road to Baddingsgill, turn right and follow the track for half a mile north, and then down left on a footpath, over a bridge, and up the far side to the road.

*Starting along the farm track*

Otherwise turn left and take the signed vehicular track, partly fenced, through fields for 4 miles, to join the main road one third of a mile south of the car park.

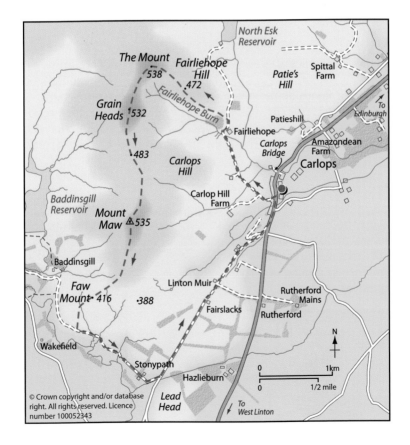

43

# 10.    Tinto West Ridge

## Character

Tinto (707m) stands isolated between the wide Upper Clyde valley on the east and the M74 corridor on the west. It is, and has been, 'iconic' for many people - witness the huge Bronze Age cairn, visible for many miles, also the broad eroded track which scars the over-popular route from the north - and snow on this track is rapidly pounded to ice.

Tinto has a long east ridge, an even longer west ridge, and a steep stepped south ridge surmounted by loose scree which is geologically important.

The West Ridge Route follows little-used grass tracks to the summit from the end of a minor road, and descends by a heather plateau and slopes, then rough pasture, to the minor road. Alternatively, return by the same route.

## Summary

| | | | |
|---|---|---|---|
| **Distance:** | 10 miles | **Height gained:** | 500m |
| **Time:** | 5 hours | **Map:** | O.S. Landranger 72 |

**Start and finish:** Roadside parking by minor road to Howgate Mouth. GR 923 358. Turn off the A73 at Fallburn (GR 966 378) and take the minor road past the popular route car park, then after 4 miles, turn left at a T junction and find the parking after half a mile on the right, by a gate to a forestry road (Do not obstruct it!)

## Route

Continue up the road (surfaced as far as Howgate) for 1 mile to the summit of the pass at Howgate Mouth, with steep ground and then disused quarries on the left.

*A winter ascent*                *Start and finish*

*Looking back -*
*Gordon Gove near Howgate Mouth*

44

*The footpath from Howgate Mouth*

*The stile*

*Lochlyoch Hill*

Immediately before the quarries, ascend a steep footpath in a groove, then cross a ricketty stile. Turn right and follow the crest of a broad ridge, on a faint track through rough grass, beside a fence and dike enclosing a plantation.

The fence and dike continue from the far end of the plantation over Lochlyoch Hill (529m), with the grass track alongside, dipping to 480m and rising to 530m, levelling, then rising steeply to the summit of Tinto.

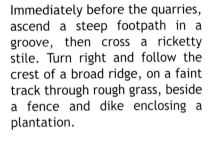

*The way to the summit*

*The summit cairn and Trig. pillar*

45

*The plateau in September*

From the huge summit cairn, observe the fence running down a little east of north with the main path beside it. Take a course diverging from this fence by about 40 degrees (about 25 from grid north), following the crown of the plateau, on short grass and heather, with very faint tracks.

*The descent*

As the ground drops, it forms a broad ridge falling away and swinging north-west. The nose of the ridge becomes steep, with deep heather and boulders, leading down towards a grass track finishing at a house. Better to use one of the narrow paths slanting down through the heather on the north flank, then cross the east edge of the fields to the minor road, where you turn left, and so back to the car.

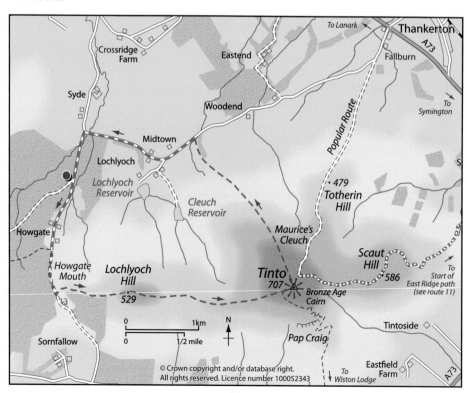

## Character

(See also under previous Route.) Seen from the north, the skyline of the east ridge suggests the perfect ascent, and seen from the east, a track may be discerned most of the way. Yet it is hardly used. The problem is access: my SMC 'Corbetts' guidebook (ISBN 0 907521 29 0) mentions a route, and indicates a small parking area, but driving along the A73, you look in vain. Presumably it is fenced off. Parking is difficult but possible, and the route is good, consisting mostly of a firm track through heather, with a surface of short grass, and fine views. Unfortunately, it is a there-and-back walk unless extra transport can be arranged, because the routes on Tinto are radial and the main road round the east would not be a pleasant walk.

## Summary

| | | | |
|---|---|---|---|
| **Distance:** | 6 miles | **Height gained:** | 480m |
| **Time:** | 3.5 hours | **Map:** | O.S. Landranger 72 |

**Start and finish:** Limited parking is possible on a grass verge beside Westside Road, a minor road off the A73 near Symington. GR 985 346.

## Route

Cross the main road with care and step through a gate into a field with a shelter belt on your left. Beware of cattle, particularly cows with young. Walk along beside the shelter belt and through a gate on the far (upper) side of the field.

*Looking down the route across the A73 to Westside Road*

Now take a narrow path slanting to the right up a steep pasture to a gate in a horizontal fence abutting another shelter belt.

*Path slanting right*

Go through the gate to cross the crest of a gentle ridge, and see ahead the clear grass track rising from the right and swinging ahead up the main east ridge.

*The gate*

*The track up the east ridge*

Continue ahead on a grass path through the heather, to join the track, and follow it as it makes a rising traverse to the right below the brow of Scaut Hill (586m), an outlier of Tinto.

*Looking back down the east ridge*

*The rising traverse*

There is only a little erosion, on the steepest gradients, so the ascent is pleasant under-foot. The track swings over the top of Scaut Hill past a prehistoric cairn, and continues along the crest of a broad ridge with a drop of only 20m.

*Tinto and Pap Craig*

There are good views of the south ridge of Tinto with the step of Pap Craig, a distin-guishing mark for distant views from east and west.

*The gate and the eroded section*

*The summit cairn from the west*

The track swings right to make a slanting ascent of the east shoulder of Tinto then through a gate in a fence and steeply up left in a short eroded section, to join the main route 180m from the summit.

Return by the same route, unless transport arrangements have been made for some other descent eg. a cycle left at Wiston Lodge below the South Ridge.

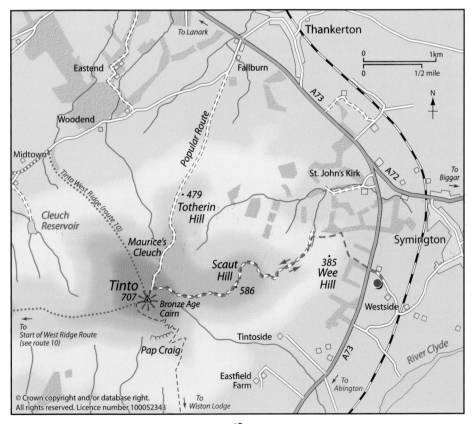

# 12.    Peebles - The Old Drove Road

## Character
The Old Drove Road running south from Peebles starts along a sharp ridge on the east side of Glen Sax and continues over bleak heathery hills. By using the estate road for 3 miles up Glen Sax and then a track up the flank of the hill, and following the ridge north, this route includes the most scenic part, with panoramic views ahead. The route could of course, be reversed, but note that if continuing along the ridge, the path marked on the OS Map down to the head of Glen Sax is completely overgrown in deep heather.

## Summary
**Distance:**     7 miles                    **Height gained:**   480m
**Time:**          4 hours                    **Map:**                 O.S. Landranger 73
**Start and finish:** Lay-by at the end of the public road  running south-east from the Tweed bridge (Springhill Road off B7062 soon after bridge, becoming Glen Road.) GR 260 393.

## Route
From the end of the public road immediately past the car parking turn right through gate pillars along the Glensax Estate road.

*Start and finish*

*The Glensax Estate road*

Following this road, keep to the right of the stream and the landscaped fishing pool, along the main track passing Newby and Upper Newby, then 2 felled plantations above on the right.

At the far end of the second plantation, a track slopes down to a ford and rises up the hill slope on the far side.

*The ford in springtime*

Cross this ford and follow the track up the slope. (A narrow plank bridge was observed a little downstream, but I would not guarantee its permanence or safety!)

The track maintains a moderate gradient and is easy underfoot, comprising mainly short grass on a firm base, almost all the way to the ridge track where it forms a 'Y' junction in rough grass.

*Looking back to the main track*

*The ascent continues*

(Note if reversing the route - look for the descent near the metal gate in the ridge fence.)

*Turn left in front of this gate*

51

Turn left along the rough ridge track and follow it beside the fence (with a plantation beyond) to the summit of Kirkhope Law (537m). Follow the track northwards, and continue across the brow of Kailzie Hill where the fence swings off right.

*North from Kirkhope Law*

Continue down to enter a wide strip of heather with a mainly grass track between two old stone walls (presumably intended to channel the drovers' cattle) following the crest of an undulating ridge.

*Craig Head*

*Into the parallel walls*

The parallel walls continue into a pronounced dip with the final sharp summit of Craig Head rising in front of you. The walls diverge: the left-hand wall follows up and along the ridge, and the right-hand wall dips around the east flank.

The walls meet again at the north end of the ridge. The main path follows the lower wall, but a good grass path also follows the ridge crest, allowing fine views on either side - across Glen Sax to the west and over the Tweed Valley to the east, as well as (after the summit) over Peebles.

*Looking back to Craig Head and the path convergence*

*Part of the descent*

*The bridge*

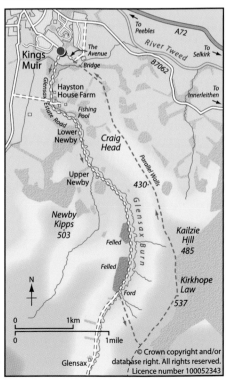

*The avenue*

After a gate the parallel walls resume, descending through pastures and woodland.

Next, follow a fence beside a field to reach a descent down a stairway through woodland, to a bridge over the stream which issued in Glen Sax. Across the stream, a beaten earth path leads to a broad avenue rising to the public road end.

# 13.        Broughton - Trahenna Hill

## Character
The traverse of a miniature Beinn a'Ghlo, on broad undulating ridges with splendid views, and unlike many Border hills, only a tiny patch of bog on top.

## Summary
**Distance:**       7 miles          **Height gained:**   375m
**Time:**           3.5 hours        **Map:**             O.S. Landranger 72
**Start and finish:** The village of Broughton: large car park behind the village hall. (Left and immediately right if approaching from Biggar.) GR 113 367.

## Route
Walk about 50m north along the main road, and turn to the right up the little road passing to left of Broughton Place (a spectacular building designed by Basil Spence in 1938 in the style of a 17th century tower house).

*Start and finish*

*Broughton Place*

Passing a cottage, continue along the grassy track (part of the John Buchan Way) and eventually, when past the end of the hill with the pass visible ahead, turn off to the right, leaving the track here.

There is a patch of bog – by-pass this by turning sharply right.

Then straight up the steep slope to join a ridge track.

*Hammer Head from the John Buchan Way in winter*

54

*The ridge track to Hammer Head*

(This slope is the only part of the walk which is remotely testing!)

The ridge track rises to the left to reach the path to the summit of Hammer Head (513m).

A hollow immediately beyond the summit usually affords good wind shelter.

*Looking back along the ridge - winter*

*Dougal Roy at the summit cairn*

Next, continue on the undulating grass track along the ridge for half a mile to a right turn of the fence. Keep to the track along this fence, then turn left at the next fence junction across a slight dip (a grass track cuts the corner) to the last and highest top of Trahenna marked by a post (549m).

*Looking back along the ridge - summer*

You pass a patch of cotton grass, beautiful in season.

Now, pathless on short turf, descend the broad slope towards the farm of Dreva.

*View south from the highest top*

*Laura Newbury on the descent*

The slope eases, and then at the end of an old dike, rises a little in a slight crest swinging to the right. Follow this crest to pass above and beyond the farm.

*The crest swinging right*

Continue above a field fence (on the right) to suddenly approach the minor road close in front of the rocky 'fort and settlement'. Strike across to the gate immediately in front of the fort, and turn right through the gate on to the minor road.

Follow this quiet road to Broughton, and immediately before the main street junction, find a gate on the right leading you behind a row of houses and the Village Hall, into the car park.

(A guidebook takes you down to the old railway, but I found it partly overgrown and unpleasant.)

*The fort and settlement*

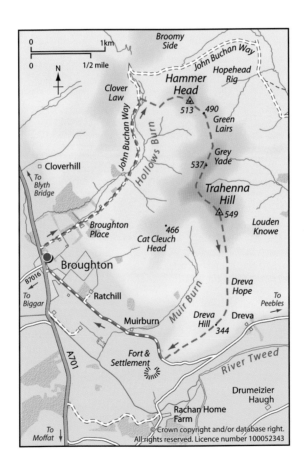

# 14.        Culter Fell from Glen Holm

## Character
A scenic approach and an interesting route, mainly on little-used grass tracks, to a popular summit.

## Summary
**Distance:**      5 miles              **Height gained:**   470m
**Time:**           3.5 hours           **Map:**             O.S. Landranger 72
**Start and finish:** Parking on grass at the end of the public road near Glenkirk farm in Glen Holm. GR 079 295 (Turn off the A701 1 mile south of Broughton.)

*Culter Fell and Chapelgill Hill from the east, with the tongue descending from the saddle*

*The twin knolls with Chapelgill Hill beyond*

## Route

The map shows a narrow ridge descending south-eastwards from the broad saddle north of the summit of Culter Fell (748m). The ridge flattens on descent and broadens into a wide tongue ending abruptly in twin knolls above the flat fields of Glen Holm. The knolls are separated by a steep little gully. This tongue and ridge form the feature used by the route.

*Parking, with Glenkirk House and Farm, and Congrie Hill beyond*

The public road up the pleasant valley of Glen Holm to Glenkirk continues past the house as a vehicular track. Follow it to pass the nearer steeper knoll of Congrie Hill, as far as the gate on the approach to the cottage of Holms Waterhead.

*Holms Waterhead*

*The author on the little hump   Photo: Sarah Newbury*

Here, cross the field to right towards the further knoll. Turn left behind the next field, crossing the foot of the steep little gully, then ascend a steep grass track. On the shoulder, the track deteriorates into twin tyre marks through coarse wet pasture, but then re-asserts itself on approaching the neck between the steep drop to Glenharvie Burn on the left, and Hope Burn on the right.

Ascend steeply over a little hump, and continue as the grass track veers to the right over the brow of the ascent towards the saddle on the main ridge. As the summit of Culter Fell is above to the left, this is clearly the 'wrong' way.

*Looking down the ridge*

Therefore, a compromise judgement must be made between diverting too far before reaching the track along the rim of the broad saddle, and over-extending the crossing of the intervening tussocky shoulder.

*The final descent. Holms Waterhead in the distance*

On the broad saddle, the grass track to the left approaches the boundary fence, then a wide braided path, slightly eroded, rises steeply to the summit, which is marked by a Trig. pillar beside the fence.

This expedition is unusual because I recommend returning the same way: the route is even more scenic in descent, and better I think, than the alternatives, indicated below.

## Other routes on Culter Fell

1. Having ascended by my recommended route, a descent may be made down the broad peaty ridge to south, then turning left down the wide tussocky slopes of Leishfoot Hill (grass tracks may be found), then a track into the valley bottom past Holms Waterhead.

2. Culter Fell may be included in the horseshoe of the head of the Glen Holm by way of Coomb Hill and Gathersnow Hill (688m), but I found this side of Gathersnow, and the head of the valley, peaty and dreary, and Coomb Hill is better combined with hills to its north-east. (See separate route description.)

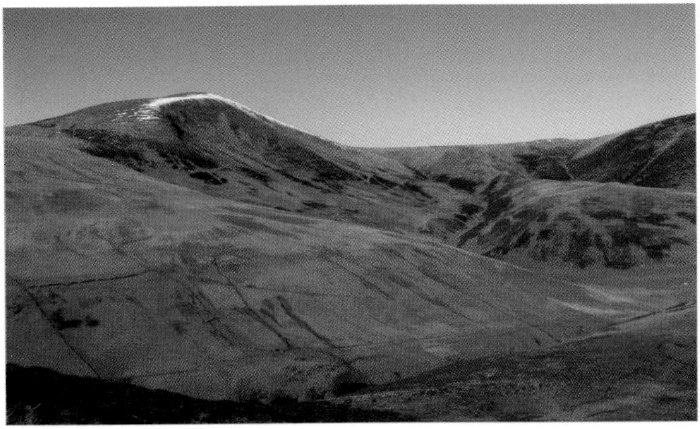

*Culter Fell from Coomb Hill showing the slopes of Leishfoot Hill*

3. A descent may also be made to the north, by returning to the broad saddle, and following near the edge of the plateau ridge on grass tracks over King Bank Head and round the deep head of the Hope Burn to the summit of Chapelgill Hill, then down a long steep slope and through a gate to cross a field to the car. I found this circuitous and less interesting than the ascent route.

4. The more usual ascent of Culter Fell is made from the west, starting at roadside parking about 1 mile south of the village of Coulter, and taking a peaty path over the broad ridge and plateau of Tippet Knowe to the saddle on my preferred route. After this approach, a return may be made by descending south-west from the summit, then taking an eroded track to the dam at Culter Waterhead. The reservoir is bereft of trees, and bleak.

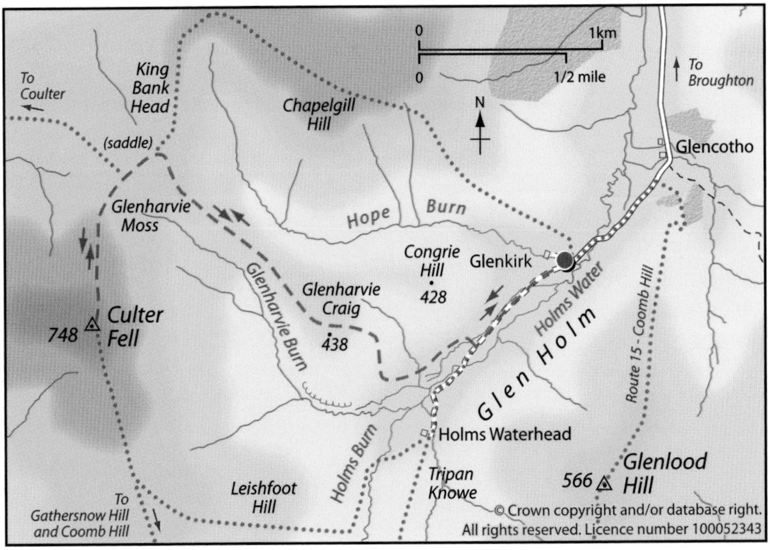

# 15.  The Round of Coomb Hill

## Character
This walk has splendid sloping ridges for the initial ascent and final descent, and a humped traverse with views of the sculptured east flanks of Culter Fell, and down Glen Holm, and a panorama of multiple hills across the Upper Clyde Valley to the east. Unfortunately, nearby wind turbines make a surgical intrusion on the east side.

## Summary
| | | | |
|---|---|---|---|
| **Distance:** | 6 miles | **Height gained:** | 480m |
| **Time:** | 4 hours | **Map:** | O.S. Landranger 72 |

**Start and finish:** In Glen Holm, at either the end of the public road as for Culter Fell, GR 079 293, or on the grass verge near Glencotho. GR 083 298.

## Route
Starting from the public road end at Glenkirk, walk along the vehicular track past the house, and continue, to pass to the left of the cottage of Holms Waterhead, and ascend a grass track on the right-hand side of a fence up the spine of a steep whaleback.

*Holms Waterhead and the whaleback*

Following this ascent, the track continues, now quite soggy in places, over level ground and up another slope.

*Level ground, then another slope*

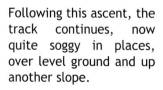

62

Then, over the brow, the track, which is now more dry, veers off right to dip slightly, then rises gently over the north shoulder of the summit of Coomb Hill (640m).

Follow the track until it levels out to bypass the summit, and strike off left at a right angle over the last few metres of mossy ground to the top, marked by a cairn of large rocks beside a fence.

*Looking back*

*The summit of Coomb Hill*

*The track levels.*
*Gathersnow Hill in sight*

*The summit cairn.*
*The Broad Law hills in the distance*

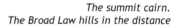

From the cairn, follow the fence descending gently to the north-east. The going becomes tussocky. Where the fence takes a sharp turn to the right, continue on the previous line until a faint grass track is discernable some 20-30 metres away from the fence, running downhill roughly parallel with it. The slope becomes very steep, and the track slants to the right to join the fence at the bottom of a dip.

*Descending gently north-east*

*Broomy Law and Glenlood Hill from the faint grass track*

*The fence takes a sharp turn right*

(In thick mist, it would be safer to follow the fence for guidance down the steep tussocky slope to the dip.)

Now follow clear wheelmarks up a heather slope near the fence to pass the top of Broomy Law (approx 550m).

*Looking back on the steep slope. The track follows the cleared slanting strip*

If visiting the unmarked summit, it is advisable (in clear weather) to return to the track immediately, as in descending the north slope through deep tussocks, it veers away from the fence to the next dip. A huge wind turbine rises from the east flank of the hill beyond the fence.

*Glenlood Hill from Broomy Law*

Now the track rises up a heathery slope to the north, near the fence, and levels out on the boggy summit of Glenlood Hill (566m).

*'the ridge narrows'*

*'a little wet in places'*

Continue over the summit beside the fence, descending slightly, and then where the fence turns sharply down the east flank, carry on along the broad gently descending ridge on a clear grass track, a little wet in places.

The ridge narrows but continues to descend steadily towards a clump of pine trees marking the foot. Just before the trees, the track steepens and turns right, then left, and then right again through the trees. Beware the slippery roots surfacing on the track.

*The track turns left*

Where the track takes its last turn right, continue down the final slope through the trees and over a few metres of pasture to the unfenced road and parked car, or if the car has been left at the public road end, walk the last half mile of road to find it.

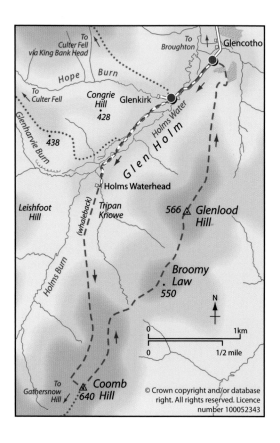

# 16.      The Round of Blakehope Head

## Character
A short walk above a secluded valley on grassy paths and tracks with a stretch of minor road, and passing a prehistoric fort and settlement.

## Summary

| | | | |
|---|---|---|---|
| **Distance:** | 4 miles | **Height gained:** | 320m |
| **Time:** | 2.5 hours | **Map:** | O.S. Landranger 72 |

**Start and finish:** In Glen Holm, 2.5 miles from the A701. Drive over a cattle grid immediately past a plantation, and find firm level grass on the left. GR 088 314.

## Route
Cross a tiny stream, and walk up a steep pasture to the bottom left-hand corner of a small plantation. Now head up left above a patch of broken ground, and find a narrow sheep path running diagonally left up the flank of the broad ridge descending to the north-west from Middle Head.

*The start and the corner of the small plantation*

*The narrow path*                           *The path continues*

The path persists on the same line up the pastures and into heather and rough grass, then fades.

*The path fades*

Now strike out uphill over the brow, and find a grass track leading leftwards to the fence on the main ridge passing over the summit of Middle Head (519m).

Turn left along the fence on a barely visible track down a slight dip, then up rather more clearly through heather to the summit of Blakehope Head (542m).

*View to the north*

From the summit, descend a rough grass track through heather north-eastwards along a fence towards the right-hand edge of a plantation.

Do not be tempted to turn down the slope to the left, because the shoulder of open hill ground is merely a bay in the upper edge of the planta-tion.

*To Middle Head summit*

*Blakehope Head from Middle Head*

*North from Blakehope Head*

Continue down a corridor between the fence on the right and the plantation on the left, to reach a substantial timber fence with a stile.

*The stile*

Ahead is open hill ground, with a low heathery hump, from which a broad ridge descends to the north-west, at a right angle to the route you have followed, and towards Glen Holm. This is the way down.

The corner may be cut and the rise avoided by traversing through tussocky grass on vague paths, to join a broad grass track, which is waymarked and runs straight down the crown of the broad ridge.

*Descending to the fort*

*The fenced field and the corner of the small plantation*

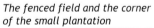

After a steady descent, the ridge rises in a broad knoll, occupied by the concentric rings of former ramparts and ditches of a prehistoric fort and settlement in a commanding position above Glen Holm.

Descend steeply from the fort, and swing left, outside the corner of a fenced field in the valley bottom. Swing left again on rough pasture to pass the corner of a small plantation, and so to the road.

Turn left along the road, to reach the parking place after about half a mile.

*The finish*

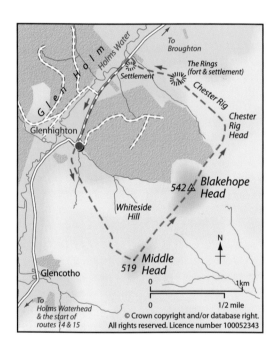

# 17.  Pykestone Hill and Drumelzier Law

## Character
Pykestone Hill is a high point (737m) on the north-south plateau ridge on which runs the former Thief's Road, and Drumelzier (pronounced 'Drumeelyer') Law (668m) is an isolated outlier to the north-west with steep heathery flanks and long sprawling approach ridges making it relatively inaccessible. This route makes use of a vehicular track to near the top of Pykestone, then intermittent grass paths and tracks to complete the circuit over Drumelzier Law.

## Summary
| | | | |
|---|---|---|---|
| **Distance:** | 9 miles | **Height gained:** | 730m |
| **Time:** | 5.5 hours | **Map:** | O.S. Landranger 72 |

**Start and finish:** The hamlet of Drumelzier. Turn off the B 712 up a lane past the houses, then left on to a grass parking area bounded by a hedge. GR 136 340.

## Route
Continue along the track past farm buildings and across a field, then between fences with a stream below on the left, and then between the stream and a steep heathery hillside.

*The track across a field*

The track dips down to the stream and crosses by a vehicular plank bridge, then fades as it rises up closely cropped grass and passes between two small plantations.

*The heathery hillside*

71

*The cluster of ruined walls and the flank of Drumelzier Law*

Immediately after the plantations, swing right and then left as the track re-asserts itself to pass a cluster of ruined walls.

Now the track forms a firm strip of short grass rising through deep heather and making ideal walking.

This is followed by a section of track which was at one time gouged by deep gullies, but has recently been regraded, making a stony surface which, being apparently stable, will hopefully re-vegetate.

*'ideal walking': looking back to the two plantations*

*The regraded track*

The gradient slackens, and a fork appears, the track to the right apparently heading for the domed summit but swinging to the south of it, and the track to the left apparently heading too far north.

Take the left-hand track. It fades to slight ruts through short heather, and swings gradually to the right, to approach the summit from about 10 degrees west of north.

*'ruts through short heather'*

*South from the summit*

On the summit plateau, the track fades as it crosses patches of turf, but the summit fence appears on a converging line, then the Trig. pillar beside it.

*'pools and tussocks'*

From the summit, follow the fence south on a narrow path through short heather and turf, gently down into a dip of pools and tussocks.

Then on sketchy paths through rough ground, continue along the fence over the slight rise of Grey Weather Law, and another slight dip and rise to a fence junction on Long Grain Knowe.

*Gordon Gove at the shepherds' cairn*

Turn right along the fence running about 20 degrees north of west for about 600m with another slight dip and rise to the top of Middle Hill. Here the fence turns to the south-west, but you strike off along the crown of a broad plateau-ridge about 10 degrees west of north to a pillar-like 'shepherds' cairn' 600m away. (In clear weather the corner may be cut from Long Grain Knowe, but the ground is very rough.)

*Drumelzier Law from Glenstiven Dod*

Continue for 140m of short grass and moss on almost level ground to the highest point of Glenstivon Dod, and the steep hump of Drumelzier Law appears to the north-west (except in mist).

'an expanse of deep heather'

On a rough path through heather descend steeply to a saddle at about 575m, and ascend to the summit ridge of Drumelzier Law. There are two cairns: the higher is at the north end.

Descend to the north-west, steeply at first, then more gently over an expanse of deep heather (unless recently burnt), using paths and tracks which form little more than furrows.

The expanse narrows to a broad ridge swinging slightly to run north, and rises a little to Logan Head (471m).

Down Finglen Rig

'grassy ways'

From Logan Head, it is possible to follow tracks leading north and then down to the north-east, but I recommend turning to the north-east here and following the double wheelmarks through the heather down the crest of Finglen Rig.

Down to the main track

This track runs out into mixed grass, heather and bracken above the plank bridge used in the ascent. Find grassy ways down to the right, then turn left outside the corner of a field, and descend steeply through heather to the main track where it emerges from the fenced section. Turn left through the gate and so back to Drumelzier.

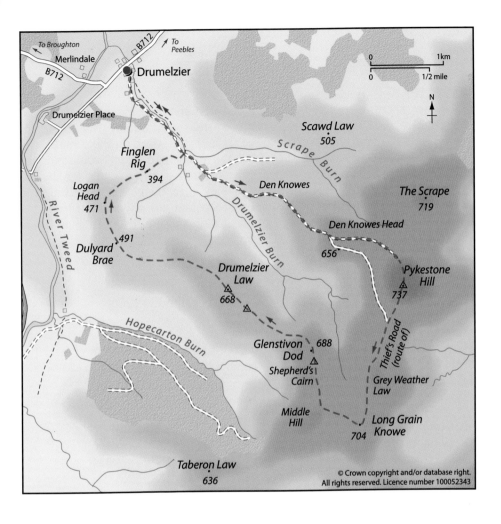

To Broughton
Merlindale
B712
B712
To Peebles
Drumelzier
Drumelzier Place

Scawd Law
505
Scrape Burn

Finglen Rig
394

Logan Head
471

Dulyard Brae
491

Den Knowes
Drumelzier Burn

Den Knowes Head
656

The Scrape
719

Pykestone Hill
737

Drumelzier Law
668

Glenstivon Dod
688
Shepherd's Cairn

Hopecarton Burn

Middle Hill

Thief's Road (route of)

Grey Weather Law

Long Grain Knowe
704

River Tweed

Taberon Law
636

0        1km
0        1/2 mile
N

# 18.    The Round of Broad Law

## Character
Broad Law (840m) is usually 'bagged' by a there-and-back expedition from the high point of the Megget Stone at 452m. on the south, but by using the engineered track through the forestry to the radio installations on the summit, the much greater ascent and distance from the main road near Tweedsmuir (to north-west) can be overcome, and a return made over a fine long ridge, by the route described here. The track is less ugly than might be expected, the summit installations stand on a small plateau and are only visible from the immediate vicinity (or, of course, from far away) and the return ridge is scenic and mostly quite good underfoot.

## Summary
**Distance:**    9.5 miles        **Height gained:**   720m
**Time:**        5.5 hours        **Map:**             O.S. Landranger 72
**Start and finish:** Lay-by on the east side of the A701 Edinburgh - Moffat road, immediately before the bridge over the Tweed accessing the farm of Hearthstane. Avoid blocking access to the communal bins in the same lay-by. GR 110 261.

## Route
Cross the bridge and walk along the straight road passing cottages on the right. Turn left across the bridge over the Hearthstane Burn, and right to follow the road past farm buildings. (Beware farm dogs, cattle, reversing tractors etc!)

*Start and finish*

*The road at the start, and the final descent*

76

Then the road runs along the edge of plantations, with views to the right across to open hillsides and the return ridge. After about half a mile, you pass a vehicular bridge and shortly after, the road rises into the forest and so continues to the gate in the top fence, with some recent fellings on the right opening the views. Poles on either side assist vehicular access to the radio installations in times of deep snow.

*'along the edge of plantations'*

The road through the forest

The gate in the top fence

After the gate, the road maintains a steady gradient for about a mile, slackening after that. At first, it is mostly well surfaced in close-cropped grass, then it becomes stony, but still quite good underfoot. The topside overhangs, which disfigure so many bull-dozed hill tracks, are not too bad.

*'mostly surfaced in close-cropped grass'*

View from the road

The road higher up

Looking back on the 'mushroom' and Trig. pillar

Almost at the top, a main junction appears. Turn right to pass a mushroom-shaped structure and reach a fence. Turn right again along this fence heading south-west, and in a few metres reach a Trig. pillar.

The fence turns almost due south. Follow it on rough, slightly soggy grass, down the very gentle plateau slope, for 1.5 miles. There are wheel marks scarcely showing, and little sign that this is part of the 'trade route' from the Megget Stone except that you may see other walkers.

South from Broad Law

*The ridge as far as Talla Cleuch Head*

Now, unless the weather is misty, you will see the start of the return ridge turning off sharply to the north-west – but I would caution against attempting to cut the corner, because of hidden gullies and peat hags which feed into the deeply cut headwaters of the Hearthstane Burn. It may be best to keep going south until the cross fence running west and then north-west is reached.

Follow this ridge fence north-west on rough grass with intermittent grass tracks, and splendid views over Talla and Games Hope.

*Looking across to Games Hope*

78

*North-west from Mathieside Cairn*

From a slight dip, ascend about 70m to the highest point in the ridge, Talla Cleuch Head (690m) -see 'The Southern Uplands' SMC Guide (ISBN 0 907521 38X). It is not named on the OS Landranger Map.

An almost level crest of easy walking runs north and then north-west to the knobbly rock summit of Mathieside Cairn (669m).

From the summit, turn away from the fence and strike off downhill due north for about 400m, then about 20 degrees west of north, down the long steep-sided steadily descending whaleback of Snout Hill.

*Down to Snout Hill*

*'The ridge flattens...'*

*The top of Hog Hill*

After Snout Hill the ridge flattens, the ground becomes rougher, and soggy in the dips, and the grass paths and tracks fade away. A choice may be made between continuing along the ridge following the forest edge, or dropping about 100m to the track running along the Hearthstane Burn.

If you use this track, it is best to cross the burn by the vehicular bridge noted earlier to return to the farm, because the track on the south side of the burn swings uphill round the end of the ridge to serve the plantations on the west side.

Continuing along the ridge, there is a slight final rise through rough grass to the top of Hog Hill (486m), then the reward of a fine panorama of the upper Tweed valley on the steep descent, with the going becoming easier underfoot.

Cross the contouring track, then an old dike, and finally a field (using the gates and avoiding livestock) to enter a farm road where you turn right and pass the cottages, then left to reach the bridge over the Tweed and the parking.

*The upper Tweed Valley from Hog Hill*

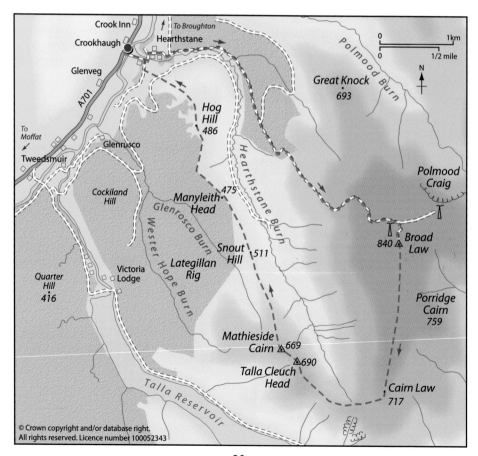

# Games Hope

## Character

Games Hope is a wild valley which descends to the head of the Talla Reservoir. The route goes up the valley by a track, crosses the stream to Gameshope Bothy, ascends by rough slopes to Garelet Dod (698m) at the southern end of the broad ridge on the west side of the valley, and returns along the ridge over Erie Hill (690m) and Garelet Hill (680m), before making a long steep descent to a bridge near the parking place.

The Gameshope Burn is powerful: the crossing to the bothy may be made almost dryshod when the water is low; but requires a wade when full: and would require the protection of an upstream rope when in spate. The final descent would require ice-axe protection on wet snow, and ice-axe and crampons on hard snow. Parts of the route are rough, parts easy. It penetrates wild country.

## Summary

**Distance:** 6 miles      **Height gained:** 640m
**Time:** 4.5 hours      **Map:** O.S. Landranger 72 & 78
**Start and finish:** From the A701 take the minor road along Talla Reservoir, and at the end, stop before the bend which starts the steep ascent to Megget, and park on the wide right hand verge. GR 134 202.

*Park before the bend which starts the ascent to Megget*

*Talla Cleuch Head from Games Hope - winter and summer*

## Route

Walk through the gate ahead and up the track with the stream on the right. The track is part eroded, part grassy. Where the valley steepens, the stream plunges among large rocks. Then the valley floor flattens, and the track ends at a corrugated iron shed, with a well-renovated bothy over the water, which should be crossed here!

*The stream by the track*

Do not be tempted to look further upstream for easier crossings - there are none near, and the going along the bank is atrocious!

*The best crossing - stream low and stream quite full; bothy shows in summer photo*

Gameshope Bothy is well equipped with basics and lovingly maintained, but there are no obvious paths in the vicinity.

*Crossing the stream higher up: Dougal Roy using 'Dry Walker' polythene waders*

*Wall plaque in the bothy*

IN MEMORY OF **ANDREW JENSEN**
14th May 1974 - 31st May 2002

WHO SADLY DIED ON SGURR THEARLAICH, ISLE OF SKYE

THIS BOTHY HAS BEEN ESTABLISHED WITH ASSISTANCE FROM THE
ANDREW JENSEN MEMORIAL FUND

" *May his spirit walk on forever ... ... ...* "

From the bothy a left-slanting way can be found to the brow of the hill above a rocky nose. The slope eases and then levels until a substantial dike and fence appear ahead. Cross with care to the grass track on the far side, and turn left (south-west) to follow the track on gently rising ground, and where it levels, strike off for about 100m to the north-west for the highest point of Garelet Dod, set in the middle of wild country.

*'A left-slanting way...'*

Return along the grass track, and continue north to a dip in the broad ridge.

*Towards Erie Hill*

*View south-east from Garelet Dod*

The track bends left and rises quite steeply, still following the dike and fence towards the summit of Erie Hill. About two-thirds of the way up, the wall and fence turn off at a right angle on to a contouring line, but a narrow path continues to the summit. It is easier to complete the ascent rather than to contour, because the contouring track soon rises, and any paths from it end in tussocky ground.

From the summit of Erie Hill, descend northwards on fairly rough ground to a dip. Continue on intermittent grass paths up the long gently rising ridge of Cairds Cleuch Rig (684m).

*At the Trig. pillar on Garelet Hill*

Continue with a slight dip and rise, and cross a dike to the summit of Garelet Hill, which is marked by an eroded Trig. pillar.

From the summit begin the descent of the east slope, trending a little to the right of the fall line to take you past the top of the big waterfall which emerges where the ground steepens. Now go down diagonally right on a

*Descent, showing the two streams*

slope which requires care, especially where the grass is short. A stream is seen on the right. Cross this at a convenient point before it steepens into waterfalls, and follow an old fence going directly downhill.

Where the slope eases, turn left and cross the streams below waterfalls then descend the lowest slopes to reach a bridge and the parking.

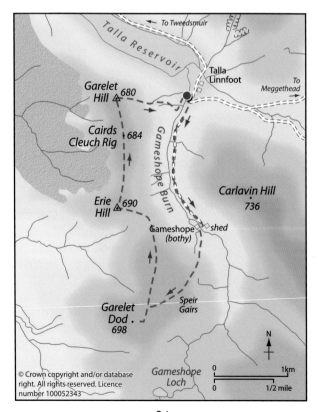

84

# 20. Moffat Hills - The Round of Capel Fell

## Character
An intensely varied and in places dramatic walk. There is a stream crossing and a section of path which, though a right of way, is potentially dangerous - **see below.**

## Summary
| | | | |
|---|---|---|---|
| **Distance:** | 8 miles | **Height gained:** | 580m |
| **Time:** | 5 hours | **Map:** | O.S. Landranger 78 & 79 |

**Start and finish:** Selcoth near Moffat. Take the Selkirk Road from Moffat and after about 5 miles, turn right through a strip of trees and across a river. Park beside the unfenced gravel road, say by the first junction, after checking at one of the houses. GR 138 078.

## Route
Walk south-west along the track, past a modern bungalow and a small plantation, and turn left at a sign, up a track before the bridge over the Selcoth Burn. (The path shown on the map on the far side is non-existent for a mile or so, but could be a fallback to avoid a difficult stream crossing if the water is in spate.)

*Start and finish. Sailfoot House in background, near exit from forest. Hill on right is an outlier of Capel Fell*

Follow the zigzags of the vehicular track up the slope, passing a rickle of stones on the brow - a good viewpoint for the hills to the north. The track becomes grassy and almost fades.

*View north over Moffat Dale*

*'The track...almost fades'*

Then, approaching the ravine at a sheep-fold, a sign indicates a descent through a gate and across a ford with rough ground on both sides.

It is usually possible to cross almost dry using the stones. (Do not be tempted to continue on the north side of the ravine: the path dwindles into steep unstable ground, with loose crags round the corner!)

*The stream crossing*

Across the stream, follow the intermittent path through deep turf on a rising traverse to a gate in a fence running up the steepening slope of Croft Head.

The path beyond is narrow and thin in places, but forms a definite traverse above the steepest slopes

*'A tricky bit'*

of hard fine scree. Care is needed! And beware of places where erosion is eating into turf below the path. If the path is slippery (e.g. because of ice) it may be possible to use the turf higher up the slope.

The ravine forms an 'L' shape, and suddenly, you reach its corner, and join the Southern Upland Way near an impressive circular sheep fold. The Way, clear and well-worn, runs high above the short limb of the 'L' shaped ravine, and dips down to a distinctive bridge above cascades.

*The Southern Upland Way crosses the grass slope on the right*

*The bridge looking back*

*Gordon Gove at Ettrick Head*       *The top to the left is the outlier seen at the start*

Then the path rises gently to a boundary fence at Ettrick Head, with a stile, a gate, and a sign 'Welcome to the Scottish Borders'. The valley beyond is densely planted with Sitka spruce.

Cross the stile, and turn left up the hill to follow a sketchy path rising up a gentle sometimes slightly wet slope, then cross a fence on the brow of the hill, to the summit of Capel Fell (678m) over on the right.

The top is domed, but by walking a few metres north, you should see the forest below, on either side of a grassy promontory. Head down for this, over 'feather-bed' turf (it may be possible to find a slight wheelmark track), and take the left-hand forestry road running down from the neck of the promontory. This road makes a gentle pleasant descent, with a good walking surface, and for much of the way, the trees are well back and 'clothed' to the ground. The road steepens a little, and takes a wide zigzag in the 'wrong' direction, then suddenly emerges from the forest near the house of Sailfoot, and the start of the walk.

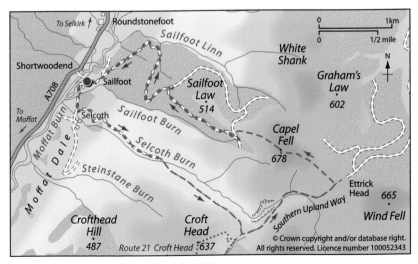

# 21. Moffat Hills – The Round of Croft Head

## Character
This route uses a section of The Southern Upland Way, returning by the waymarked Alternative Route over the summit of Croft Head.. There is the possibility that the main route may be closed during forestry operations, leaving the Alternative Route as a there-and-back walk. The walk is partly on forestry roads and paths, partly on hill paths. The start and finish below the forest is pastoral; the forest has some recent clear-fell sections, but above the forest are fine scenic views.

## Summary
**Distance:**     8 miles       **Height gained:**  530m
**Time:**          4.5 hours    **Map:**         O.S. Landranger 78 & 79
**Start and finish:** Roadside verge north of the bridge on the minor road joining the Moffat-Selkirk road 2 miles out of Moffat. GR 106 044.

## Route
Cross the bridge and turn left along the unsurfaced road signed 'Southern Upland Way' winding eastwards through fields and into the forest.

Continue along the main forestry road passing the ornate entrance to Craigbeck Hope.

*The start of the road*

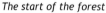
*The start of the forest*

*Craigbeck Hope*

Continue on a generally rising route, until you take a big loop to the right, round the end of an open hollow.

Here turn off left beside a stream on a built and waymarked footpath through a narrow avenue in the trees.

*The start of the path*

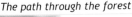
*The path through the forest*

This path is firm and dry, if a little overgrown in places. Soon the avenue and path approach the steep south-eastern slope of Croft Head, and continue, rising gently, along the foot of the slope.

Then the route reaches the forest boundary fence, which it crosses by a substantial stile, and continues by a roughly constructed footpath which approaches a renovated sheep-fold on the right, and ahead, the brink of the deep ravine of the Selcoth Burn.

*The ravine of the Selcoth Burn and the sheepfold*

Here is a sign with a map marked 'YOU ARE HERE' at the junction with the Southern Upland Way Alternative Route. Turn left here, up the grassy slope of Croft Head, on a path which becomes an ugly zigzag gash up to the brow of the hill, with eroding overhangs and protruding plastic drain pipes - but making an easy ascent. As the gradient lessens, the path continues as a thin line through the grass to the summit (637m) with a gate and marker post at the fence junction.

*The ugly path*

*The summit of Croft Head*

*View of the forestry path from the summit*

From the summit the route continues along the edge of a broad ridge, with a fence close on the right, and a steep slope affording fine views on the left.

*The ridge*

The ridge eventually flattens, the ground becomes heathery and tussocky, but the grass path remains clear and good.

*Approaching the forest*

*The steep path*

Then the ridge merges into a gentle slope with conifers ahead, and the path, now quite rough, drops down to a forest road.

Descend this road for about 700m. then at a bend (look out for the marker), drop down from the road and descend a steep grassed path.

Into a dense plantation                                    The bridge

Turn right along the road at the bottom, then off left across rough open ground and follow a substantial wall into a dense plantation, and suddenly turn left under the trees and down to a bridge over a spectacular cascade, and up to the forest road at the entrance to the forest. Then gently down the unsurfaced road to the start, with good views out over the Dale of Moffat.

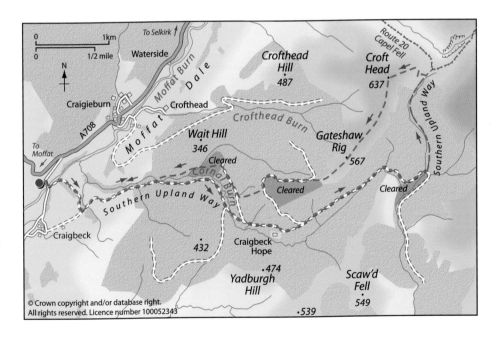

# 22.    Well Hill from Durisdeer

## Character

Well Hill forms part of a compact group of steep-sided grassy hills between the Dalveen Pass used by the A 702 Abington - Thornhill road on the west, and a pass which carried a Roman road on the east, rising from the tiny village of Durisdeer at the south end. Well Hill stands on the north-east, close to the summit of the pass. The group is deeply dissected, but the route winds to connect the ends with only a moderate loss of height, using grass tracks. The views are superb.

## Summary

**Distance:**     5.5 miles         **Height gained:** 570m
**Time:**         4 hours           **Map:**           O.S. Landranger 78
**Start and finish:** Durisdeer - park carefully in the village square. GR 894 037.
(For Durisdeer, take the Abington - Thornhill road, A 702, and turn off east on the minor road at Durisdeer Mill GR 883 042, or at GR 885 022.)

## Route

From the village square, take the short lane to right of the church, then step through a gate on to a vehicular track, which is firm but nicely grassed after the first few metres, and climbs steadily at a gentle gradient all the way to the top.

*The village square, Durisdeer*

*The track: Well Hill ahead, and the slopes of Penbane and Durisdeer Hill to left and right*

The rough slopes of Durisdeer Hill (569m) rise to the right; whilst to the left, across the valley with the grassed-over Roman fortlet, Penbane (514m) juts out between deep recesses. Ahead on the left rises Well Hill (608m).

*The gate*

At the top of the pass, a smart metal gate in a drystone wall indicates the way to Well Hill. Cross a patch of rushes, and gain the start of a footpath benched into the steep hillside and slanting up to the left.

*The benched path*

The path stops at the top of the steep lower slope.

Continue by zigzagging up the turf, trending left over the brow of the hill to join a grass track, with a wall and fence beyond. The track continues through deep turf to the summit.

*The summit of Well Hill*

From the summit of Well Hill, go through the 2 gates and return along the far side of the wall and fence using a grass track, then swing right and downhill towards Penbane, which appears almost separated from the main group of hills.

Ahead on the right is a lower outlier of Well Hill forming a broad hummocky ridge, and straight across its east flank, there emerges a horizontal fence with a grass path close above it.

*Penbane to the left and Black Hill to the right*

*The horizontal fence*

Take this path beside the fence, or alternatively the slight track along the broad ridge of the outlier, and then drop steeply and cross the fence in the boggy dip through a gate. Walk a few metres up through heather to reach a level grass track cutting across the north side of Penbane to a sharp saddle between Penbane and Black Hill.

As an optional extra, the summit of Penbane may be ascended, returning down a grass track to the saddle.

*The Penbane saddle*

From the saddle, take the grass track up Black Hill (531m). The Trig. pillar is a few metres off to the right of the main track.

From the summit of Black Hill, there is a designated public footpath to Durisdeer, running over Castle Hill (not named on the OS map) which forms the end of the range.

*Looking Back to Penbane*

*Castle Hill from the slope of Black Hill*

94